preventing and managing challenging and hazardous behaviour

A learning resource for those supporting people in care

Securicare International Ltd

Martin House, Barley Rise, Strensall, York, England, YO32 5AA.
Telephone: +44 (0) 1904 492 442
Email: trainers@securicare.com
Website: www.securicare.com

ISBN number: 978-0-9560159-2-1

Printed by Wood Richardson Ltd, Digital and Litho Printers,
Royden House, 156 Haxby Road, York, England, YO31 8EY

Copyright 2020. SecuriCare International limited.

All rights reserved. No part of this publication may be reproduced, stored in a retrieval system or transmitted in any form or by any means, electronic, mechanical, photocopying, recording or otherwise, without prior permission of SecuriCare International Limited.

Important note:

Although great care has been taken in the production of this guidance to ensure accuracy, the Publishers cannot under any circumstances accept responsibility for errors, omissions or advice given in this publication.

preventing and managing challenging and hazardous behaviour

Authors
Philip N Hardy
Stuart Godfrey
Joanne Turner

Published by
SecuriCare International Ltd

CONTENTS:

Introduction
Legislation and Guidance
Defining Challenging and Hazardous Behaviour
Primary and Preventative Strategies
Understanding and Analysing Individual Characteristics
Person Centred Planning and Positive Behavioural Support
Secondary Strategies Including De-escalation and Communication
Tertiary Strategies Including Physical Interventions
Risks of Physical Intervention Including Asphyxia
Post Incident Procedures and Support
Reflective Practice

Introduction

This booklet provides guidance for people who support and work with adults in care settings and who may experience episodes of disruptive, challenging and hazardous behaviour from those people they support. This information should help those supporting people in care to intervene in positive and pro-active ways that reduce the need for restrictive interventions.

The principles and values that underpin this guidance and advice are based on the vast experience of the authors and past and current guidance and standards including: the Department of Health Guidance: Positive and Pro-active Care (circa 2014); the Restraint Reduction Network Standards (2020); and the Institute of Conflict Management Training Standards (2020). These standards all emphasise the need to implement systems and approaches that promote positive behaviour and reduce the need for restrictive practices.

The information and advice provided will help staff and others who help in the provision of support and care to identify the causes and functions of behaviour, prevent incidents of challenging behaviour occurring, and where this is not possible help them to manage incidents in a way that prevents any further escalation and promotes positive behaviours using a person centred approach.

Why do we need this training?

Working with and supporting people can be both rewarding and challenging. It requires a person with many qualities, attributes and skills. As well as helping people live more fulfilled lives and meeting their needs, supporting people with complex needs can also present us with behaviours that are distressing, challenging and occasionally hazardous.

This can be difficult for everyone involved, including the person being supported, staff, family and anyone else present at the time. It can place staff in a position where they have to make difficult choices that can have consequences and can affect everyone involved in many ways.

To help make the right choices, to reduce distress and to support organisations, staff and those being cared for, a knowledge of the current guidance and legislation is essential.

Legislation, Regulations and Guidance

It is important to understand that when working with individuals who may at times present in a challenging, disruptive and potentially hazardous manner, we as professionals, have laws, regulations and guidance to understand and to follow for the dignity, safety and well-being of everybody involved.

Whilst there are obvious laws in place to ensure the safety of those within the care of others, there is also a duty of care owed to employees by their employer to manage the risk of violence and aggression towards staff in the workplace under occupational health and safety law.

> The Health and Safety Executive (HSE) definition of work related violence is:
>
> *"Any incident in which a person is abused, threatened or assaulted in circumstances relating to their work, involving an explicit or implicit challenge to their safety, well-being or health".*

Restraint Reduction Network (RRN) Standards (2020)

The RRN standards have been introduced to increase the focus on restraint reduction across the NHS and adult social care. It is vital that services understand and apply the principles of restraint reduction.

Physical restraint can be humiliating, terrifying and even life threatening and should only ever be used as a last resort, when there is no other way of de-escalating a situation where someone may harm themselves or others. Any restrictive intervention must be based on an assessment that intervention is likely to cause less harm than not intervening.

The standards provide a national and international benchmark for training in supporting people who are distressed.

The RRN standards are focussed on increasing understanding of the underlying root causes of behaviour and that behaviours are often displayed due to unmet needs. The standards also aim to protect people's fundamental human rights and promote person centred, best interest and therapeutic approaches to supporting people who are distressed; improve the quality of life for those being restrained and those supporting them by reducing reliance on restrictive practices; promoting positive culture and practice that focuses on prevention, de-escalation and reflective practice.

Where restrictive intervention is required, focus will then be placed on the safest and most dignified use for the shortest period of time including any physical restraint.

Human Rights Act (1998)

The Human Rights Act secures certain rights and freedoms and sets standards to be attained by everyone. With regard to the use of physical interventions, carers may be compromised from a number of perspectives. The use of physical interventions is more likely to be a breach of human rights when:
- People are subjected to pain or injury as a consequence of the method of intervention
- Where interventions are carried out in a public place, with no attempt being made to remove observers or protect the individual's dignity

- Where interventions undermine the individual's status and respect, or are degrading, or they are used as punishment or sanction
- Where interventions are used with a bias towards certain individuals because of their particular profile, needs or diagnosis (culture, religion, ethnicity, gender etc.)

Challenges may be brought against carers who use physical interventions with a service user for a period of time longer than can be legally or therapeutically justified.

It is important to follow a human rights approach such as the PANEL Framework (explained later) when supporting people.

Mental Capacity Act (2005)

The Mental Capacity Act (MCA) ensures that those individuals who, either transitorily or through long term conditions, lack the ability to understand and make informed choices are protected from having their rights interfered with. The MCA code of practice provides a statutory framework to assess and protect those who may, due to impairment or disturbance of the mind or brain, be unable to protect themselves.

Safeguarding of Vulnerable Groups Act (2006)

This legislation was passed to help avoid harm, or risk of harm, by preventing people who are unsuitable to work with children or vulnerable adults from gaining access to them through their work. It ensures that those working with vulnerable individuals are vetted by way of the Disclosure and Barring Service for any historical accounts of harm or abuse.

It is the professional responsibility of anyone working with those who may need care and support to uphold their freedom from abuse or neglect; this can be done by ensuring that their own actions do not cause harm or abuse, but also that they do not allow others to commit acts of harm or abuse. Failure to respond to any allegation or observation of abuse is equally as detrimental as committing the act oneself.

Duty of Candour

There is a statutory duty to be open and honest with service users, or their families, when something goes wrong that appears to have caused, or in the future could lead to, significant harm. Professional duty of candour is the duty of every health and social care professional to be open and honest about everything they do. Care organisations have a general duty to be open and transparent in relation to care. The duty, like the contractual one, applies to organisations rather than individuals, but staff should cooperate to make sure the organisational obligation is met.

Historical Approaches to Challenging Behaviour

Society's understanding of people and how they behave has come a long way from previous ideas and attitudes. Historically, those that were seen to be "different" would be kept isolated from mainstream society, either by being kept at home or being placed in an institution. Some common reasons why individuals would be isolated include: psychosis, schizophrenia, physical disability, epilepsy and depression.

As professionals started to learn and understand more, things began to change, ideas such as normalisation and social role valorisation were developed in the 1970's by Wolf Wolfensburger. These ideas led others to realise the importance of inclusivity and that everybody can play a valued and dignified role in society.

These were welcome changes to the institutional model which was based on control and suppression, where individuals were treated with contempt instead of compassion and care. It was the foundation from which we now stand in seeing the importance of individual identity and adopting person centred and human approaches to care and support and understand that behaviour is often driven by a desire to have needs met.

The attributes that are most important to supporting those with behaviours that may challenge and distress have changed from an authoritarian manner to include, but are not limited to, the following:
- Good communication skills, including listening and observation
- Initiative and problem solving

- Good team working
- Planning and organisation skills
- Reflective practice
- Patience and flexibility
- Compassion and empathy
- Honesty and reliability
- Emotional resilience
- A commitment to improve the quality of life for others

A Human Rights Approach

Any person receiving care and treatment must have their human rights respected (Human Rights Act (HRA) 1998) and these human rights should be at the centre of any decision making. The same human rights apply to a person's family, carers, others receiving care/treatment and all those involved in providing care and support.

Any use of lawful restrictive interventions must be rights respecting; not cause harm and protect a person's right to life. A human rights approach also means involving the person in the decision making and should be the least restrictive option.

The following are key points of a human rights approach:
- Understanding human rights in relation to the use of restrictive interventions
- Safeguarding against serious harm when using restrictive interventions
- Assuming capacity as set out in the Mental Capacity Act 2005
- Treating distress and behaviours of concern as acts of communication
- Consideration of the person's experience of restrictive intervention and its impact on their mental and physical health
- A commitment to involve those with lived experience in planning and developing their care and treatment
- Processes and practices that avoid or minimise the use of restrictive interventions

The British Institute of Human Rights PANEL Framework (2013)

This provides a set of principles that breaks down what a human rights based approach means in practice. **PANEL** stands for:

Participation
People should be involved in decisions that affect their rights. This should be at the centre of strategic planning and involve the participation of those who may be affected by any decision.

Accountability
There should be monitoring of how people's rights are being affected, as well as remedies when things go wrong. This should be informed by a rigorous evidence base drawing on our own and others research.

Non-Discrimination and Equality
All forms of discrimination must be prohibited, prevented and eliminated. People who face the biggest barriers to realising their rights will be prioritised.

Empowerment
Everyone should understand their rights, and be fully supported to take part in developing policy and practices which affect their lives.

Legality
Approaches should be grounded in the legal rights that are set out in local and international laws.

What are Challenging and Hazardous Behaviours

A commonly accepted definition of "Challenging Behaviour" is:

> "Behaviour of such an intensity, frequency or duration that the physical safety of the person or others is likely to be placed in serious jeopardy, or behaviour which is likely to seriously limit or deny access to and use of ordinary community facilities; or behaviour that is likely to impair a child's personal development and family life and which represents a challenge to services, to families and to the children themselves, however caused."
> (Emerson et al 2001)

The term challenging behaviour is used to describe a wide and varied range of behaviours which includes: distressed, difficult and problematic behaviour, absconding, tantrums, sexually inappropriate actions/comments/gestures, eating inedible objects, continual questioning, rocking or other stereotypical movements, even aggressive and violent behaviour. Characteristically, challenging behaviour puts the safety of the person and others in some jeopardy. It can have a significant impact on the quality of life of the people involved.

It is important from a risk assessment perspective that we differentiate between challenging behaviour and behaviours where there is a serious risk to well-being, safety and maybe life. These behaviours are Hazardous. It is important that any behaviour that poses a potential risk of significant harm is identified clearly to enable those supporting the person to manage the risk safely.

Hazardous Behaviours can include but is not limited to:
- Grabbing
- Hitting
- Kicking
- Biting
- Spitting
- Self-injury
- Smashing inanimate objects/property
- Throwing things

In order to prevent challenging and or hazardous behaviours, it is necessary to understand why the behaviour occurs in the first place.

Primary and Preventative Strategies

Primary and preventative strategies focus on the following key areas:
- Identifying the root causes, influencing factors and functions of behaviour; and understanding individual characteristics
- Ensuring people's needs are met so they are less likely to develop distressed or other behaviours of concern
- The use of evidenced based frameworks such as Positive Behavioural Support
- The use of person centred approaches
- Reflection and reflective practices

In order to effectively prevent and manage challenging or hazardous behaviour, we must first be able to understand why the behaviour occurs. This in turn will help us support people in ways that meet their needs, reduces distress and anxiety and helps us plan for those events that cannot be avoided so we can manage them in the least restrictive way.

Let's start by looking at why people choose to present challenging and hazardous behaviours.

Influencing Factors

There are numerous factors that may influence how a person behaves; it may be their socio-economic background, education and formative development, behavioural phenotype (see Understanding Individual Characteristics), physical or mental health, physical impairment, memories of previous life events, peer group pressure, communication difficulties, the environment, drugs or medication, alcohol or substance misuse. Other examples include but are not limited to:

- Personality disorders
- Sensory impairment
- Common frustrations
- Negative events
- Increase/decrease to sensory stimulation
- Reaction to authority
- Reaction to loss/pain
- Change of immediate environment/routine
- Tiredness/hunger
- Personal problems
- Expressions of anxiety/stress/boredom
- Fear/phobias
- Prejudice
- Personal beliefs
- Restrictions

Many of these factors are common to us all. People with complex needs will find some of these factors even more difficult to manage. There are also other wider factors to consider that can affect the lives of people we support.

Society

Society and the general public can also affect the mood or behaviour of service users. They often experience problems with people's attitudes or lack of understanding or stereotyping. They may also experience restrictions in the form of a lack of choices and/or employment opportunities, access to education and mobility. They are often restricted financially as well.

The Service

The lives of service users are also sometimes affected by the very service that was designed for their care. Timetables are often designed for the group rather than the individual, or on what the staff "think" the service user should be doing. A lack of time or resources may lead to a lack of choice or support. By making assumptions or decisions for people we could end up de-skilling some individuals.

Staff morale and attitude, or the "service culture" can all affect the lives of both service users and staff. We must avoid the "THEM" and "US" mentality and adopt an inclusive approach that is non-judgemental.

Due to the demands of service delivery, staff could be having a busy or hectic day, but in contrast, for the individual service user(s), this can be a rather dull and under-stimulating experience. Unreasonable expectations on people and services can sometimes lead to stress and changes in mood, attitude and behaviour.

You must try to stay aware and be sensitive to the needs of the service user group ("it's the little things that count"). By being conscious of your own approach, you can make a vital contribution which can make a positive difference to your service user's standard of care.

Functions of Behaviour

It is important to understand that any behaviour being displayed may not only have multiple factors behind it, but it can also be there to serve a function.

Common functions of behaviour are:
- to gain attention
- to avoid or escape a situation
- to gain access to preferred items/places/people
- to reduce anxiety or agitation in themselves
- to gain or retain power or control over their life
- as a means of communication

Identifying Causes and Triggers

Identifying the "trigger factors" to a particular behaviour will help find a solution or plan an appropriate response. Everyone has days when nothing seems to go right. People sometimes feel they have not received the service or response they had expected. This can lead to a build-up of frustration that can result in intolerance and changes to attitude and behaviour.

Setting Events

Knowing that behaviour has a function or is influenced by one or more underlying causes/factors, helps us understand why the behaviour is displayed by an individual. As well as identifying the causes and functions of behaviour, we need to gather as much information as possible including historical influences, life events and genetic factors, these setting events are referred to as slow triggers.

Slow triggers are prior events or conditions, either external or internal, which influence the probability of the individual presenting challenging behaviour. These events often happen in the distant past and are different to the triggers that are often observed just prior to a display of challenging behaviour. The slow triggers do not typically cause the challenging behaviour, but their presence makes it more likely for the behaviour to emerge. Examples of slow triggers include past experiences/abuse, life events such as bereavement, phenotype behaviour and long term physical and mental health issues.

Fast triggers are the events that occur, usually, just before the display of the challenging behaviour. They describe the influencing factors that provide the catalyst or trigger to the change in behaviour and are referred to as the antecedent.

Examples of fast triggers include, but are not limited to:
- Difficulty communicating
- Fears/phobias

- Restrictions being imposed
- Change or transitions
- An unexpected event
- Unmet needs
- Under/over stimulation

Often the people we support find stressful situation more difficult to process or manage, they may not have the understanding, ability or skill set required and may be unable to control their behavioural response.

Understanding Individual Characteristics

When developing support plans for those individuals in your care you need to look at who they are. These support plans will be unique and are based on individual characteristics such as medical diagnosis, phenotype behaviours, preferred methods of communication, understanding, information processing, preferences, sensory differences, medical conditions, mental health diagnosis etc.

When we are working with or supporting individuals with challenging behaviour, we need to be aware that each person is still an individual, they have their own attributes, abilities and characteristics that make them who they are and often how they react to situations.

There is, however, evidence that certain diagnoses lead people to behave in certain ways, for example, a person living with dementia may display symptoms of hallucination or believing they are living in a different period of their life, which when challenged about could result in an emotional outburst or an aggressive display. Another example is, an individual on the autistic spectrum may be focused on a topic or subject irrespective of lack of interest or input from others and may not be able to understand why the other person has moved on or changes the subject. These are two examples of phenotype behaviours.

Phenotype behaviours refer to those aspects of a person's behaviour that can be attributed to the presence of a specific genetic or biological anomaly or condition. We can expect people with certain conditions to have a tendency towards certain behaviours. This might mean altering the service to accommodate the behaviours. By having a deeper understanding of a person's condition, you will be better prepared for such behaviours if they arise.

Examples of Behavioural Phenotypes:

Prader-Willi Syndrome: Excessive interests in food, over eating, skin picking, and difficulties with changes of routine. Obsessive and compulsive behaviours and mood fluctuations.

Down's Syndrome: Conduct/oppositional disorders; mood fluctuations, they can have a happy mood then switch to a low mood, or a major depressive disorder; stubbornness and obsessive and compulsive behaviours. People with Down's Syndrome can also present attention deficit hyperactivity disorder.

Attention Deficit Hyperactivity Disorder (ADHD):
- **Inattentive type**: fails to give close attention; careless mistakes; appears not to listen; avoids or dislikes tasks that require sustained mental effort; easily distracted
- **Hyperactive/Impulsive type**: fidgets/squirms; difficulty remaining seated; runs around/climbs; acts as if driven by a motor; talks excessively; blurts out answers before the question has been completed; difficulty waiting/taking turns; interrupts others

Tourette's Syndrome: Obsessive compulsive phenomena; unconsciously copying behaviours (echophenomena); inappropriate swearing and making obscene gestures (coprophenomena); self-injury; attention deficit disorder; and hyperactivity or aggression.

Smith-Magenis Syndrome: Loving, caring, friendly and eager to please; a good sense of humour; impulsivity, hyperactivity; irritability and distractibility; temper tantrums; self-injury; aggression; severe sleep problems; night wakening and daytime sleepiness.

Asperger's Syndrome: A milder variant of Autism; social isolation and eccentric behaviour in childhood (eye contact/facial expressions/body postures); impaired two-sided social interaction; speech can sound peculiar due to abnormalities in inflection and repetitive patterns; clumsiness in articulation and gross motor behaviour; an interest in a specific area that prevent more appropriate age common interests.

Learning Disabilities: A learning disability is;

> *"a state of arrested or incomplete development of mind, which means that the person can have difficulties understanding, learning and remembering new things, and in applying that learning to new situations."*
> (World Health Organisation, 2015: Promoting Rights and Community Living for Children with Psychological Disabilities.)

Learning disabilities affect the way a person learns new things throughout their lifetime. They also have an impact on how the individual understands information and how they communicate.

The Department of Health includes the following in the definition of a Learning Disability:
- **Impaired intelligence**: reduced ability to understand new/complex information or learn new skills
- **Impaired social functioning**: reduced ability to cope independently

From these definitions we can understand that learning disabilities relate to intellectual disability and should not be confused with learning difficulties such as dyslexia, ADHD or dyspraxia which do not affect general intelligence.

There are two causes of learning disability:
1. **Genetic:** which may develop prior to conception or during the early stages of foetal development
2. **Environmental:** which includes external factors that may affect the development of foetus and child such as complications at birth, trauma, social deprivation

Learning disabilities are separated into 4 categories:
1. **Mild:** Difficultly in learning but can acquire daily living skills
2. **Moderate:** Considerable difficulty in learning and requires input in achieving daily living skills
3. **Severe:** Substantial difficulty in learning; limited language skills; requires support with daily living skills
4. **Profound:** Extreme difficulty in learning; limited communication skills; dependence on others for daily living skills

Around 1.2 million people in England are understood to have a form of learning disability. Most people in England living with a learning disability fall into the mild category, living independent lives with little outside support and only relying on clinical and health services in times of crisis.

Autism:

Obsessive behaviours in activities and interests. Repetitive body movements such as hand flapping, rocking and spinning. Obsessive attachments to unusual objects. A person with autism can often become upset if a routine is changed or broken.

The term Autism is made up of the words: *aut* = self; and *ism* = orientation or state. It literally means the "tendency to be absorbed in oneself"; it was first used by Leo Kanner following a study of individuals with a learning disability and identified patterns of behaviour.
The most widely accepted definition of Autism was formulated in 1978 by Lorna Wing and Judith Gould as a triad of impairments:
1. **Impairment of social relationships:** difficulty in understanding, communicating, and recognising how other people are feeling
2. **Impairment of social communication:** difficulty understanding verbal and non-verbal language
3. **Impairment of social imagination:** difficulty imagining what others are thinking or alternatives to their own routine

Autism became known as a spectrum condition because each individual with a diagnosis would exhibit signs associated with each impairment to a greater or lesser degree depending on multiple factors such as severity of learning disability, sensory impairment, learning difficulty.

Dementia:

The term Dementia is used to describe the symptoms that occur when the brain is affected by specific diseases and conditions, these include Alzheimer's disease. It can also be the result of a stroke. Dementia is progressive and the symptoms will gradually get worse. Each person is unique and will experience Dementia in their own way. The symptoms include:
- Loss of memory
- Mood changes
- Communication problems
- Emotional/behavioural changes
- Increasing dependence on others

Mental Health:

It is probably most helpful to consider mental health illness under 4 broad headings:
1. **Neuroses:** This group of disorders has excessive fear or anxiety at the root. This fear/anxiety can be quite overpowering and interrupt daily activities
2. **Mood Disorders:** This most commonly takes the form of depression; however, some people experience periods of elation/excitement known as "mania"
3. **Functional Psychoses:** Disorders of unknown cause that involve major disturbances in a person's mental life such as: Disturbed Thinking - thoughts that may be disjointed or illogical; Delusional Beliefs - a person comes to believe things about themselves or the world that are clearly not true; Hallucinations - the person hears or sees things which are not present
4. **Organic Psychoses:** Have many of the hall-marks of functional psychoses, but is linked to diseases including Alzheimer's and Parkinson's

Now we have an understanding of the possible underlying contributing factors to changes in behaviour we need to analyse this on an individual basis.

Analysing Behaviour

All the necessary information relating to a person's behaviour should be recorded and documented and be available to help us analyse why an individual presents challenging behaviour. This way of looking at behaviour and using the information to devise strategies and management plans is called functional analysis or functional assessment.

Models of functional assessment require information in three areas to help identify the elements underpinning the behaviour. Commonly referred to as ABC or behavioural charts, they are broken down into the following:
1. **Antecedent:** What was happening just before the behaviour occurred?
2. **Behaviour:** What the behaviour was? - this needs to be a detailed scaled description
3. **Consequence:** What were the consequences of the behaviour? What were the reactions? Did they gain or lose something as a result?

It is usually fairly simple to identify and record the behaviour shown by a particular service user e.g. "John grabbed Mary by the hair". One benefit of accurately recording the type of behaviour, its frequency and the impact it has, is to help organisations prioritise any corrective actions it may need to implement or amend.

Perhaps a more difficult area to address is why the behaviour occurred in the first place. Identifying the antecedent to the behaviour is the basis of good behavioural management planning. By analysing what happened just prior to the occurrence, we should be able to plan against the antecedent occurring again, or at least plan a positive response next time.

Equally important is the need to identify the consequences of the behaviour. If the outcome is that the person gets what they wanted, then it is possible the behaviour is being reinforced and may re-occur.

ABC Charts are used to identify two categories: personal and environmental factors. Each of these categories can be sub-divided into temporary and persistent factors or events.

Category	Temporary Factors	Persistent Factors
Personal	Hungry, up-set, tired etc	Learning disability, physical disability, dementia
Environmental	Hot/cold, crowded, dark etc	Location, setting/design, facilities or accessibility

When we have this information, it is fundamental that we learn from these assessments and adopt an individual person centred behavioural support plan with a human rights approach that helps to understand the behaviour and its triggers; reduce the need for restrictive interventions and improve the quality of life for the individual.

> "It is not a matter of what causes self-injury or what causes aggression or what causes stereotyped or repetitive movements but for each of these difficult forms of difficult behaviour, what does it do for the individual, what purpose does it serve for them in their life?"
> (Person centred approaches)
> E. Emerson (quote from Brown and Brown, 1994)

Developing a Person Centred Management Plan

Developing and introducing any kind of support plan takes time, it takes input from everyone involved, including the individual concerned and it should be focussed on the needs of the individual requiring support, not the service providing the support. Other people that could be included in this development are:
- Family
- Friends
- Medical professionals
- Support staff
- Key workers
- Advocates

A person centred plan needs to focus on the needs, wishes and preferences of the individual. It will be an evolving document; as the individual progresses, develops and achieves goals the plan should reflect this. Ideally this plan would be written by the individual and use the "I" as opposed to "insert name". This helps with ownership of the plan and therefore makes it relevant to them, an example may be; "When I start to feel angry I will try and speak to a member of staff that I trust", this is different to "when (name) feels angry they will find a staff member to talk to".

Information that will support the development of a good person centred plan will also include details such as:
- Referral/background information
- Service user's profile
- Physical characteristics
- Cognitive abilities
- Communication abilities
- Self-care skills
- Community, social, domestic, recreational and leisure skills
- Living arrangements
- Health & medical status

We must consider that some of the historic information may no longer reflect who the individual is at the present time, but by having access to it we can look at previous developments and use this information to inform working strategies or develop new ones that are more relevant and effective. It should also help you look for ways to promote positive behaviours.

Positive Behavioural Support

The overall aim of Positive Behavioural Support (PBS), "is to improve the quality of a person's life and that of the people around them" (Koegel & Dunlap 1996; Carr, Horner et al 1999).

PBS is a way of working with individuals whose behaviour challenges those around them and has the potential to limit their own opportunities and interactions within society. The PBS approach is about developing practical, person centred, human rights based strategies promoting values such as dignity and respect to support an individual to learn about and manage challenging behaviours to promote a positive outcome as opposed to a restrictive, negative outcome.

To begin to implement PBS driven person centred strategies we need to understand each service user's unique likes and dislikes, this includes looking at individual characteristics (covered earlier), the environment within which they live and their social needs. What modifications are required for positive involvement such as hearing loops and accessibility, how personalised is the home environment? This is easier to achieve in private spaces such as bedrooms. Where there is communal living, we should still look at how we are achieving this.

Here are some examples of techniques used to promote positive behaviours:
- **Positive reinforcement**: When a service user does something positive or helpful, we should reinforce this behaviour to encourage the person to use this behaviour again. Verbal praise and/or non-conditional time being given to this person can be the simplest form of a positive reward.
- **Modelling**: We should try to demonstrate or point out a way of behaving that the service user can imitate. In this way the service user may model their response in a similar way. Staff must act as a role model in both their behaviour and communication.
- **Cueing**: Is a stimulus (or pattern of stimuli) that results in a specific learned behavioural response. This way the stimulus, e.g. a pat on the back or a clap of the hands, becomes the cue for appropriate behaviour. Tangible items may also be used as a cue to support communication e.g. Picture Exchange Communications System (PECS), as well as pictorials/photographs of activities, items or objects.

- **Shaping**: Reinforce required responses, whilst discouraging other less appropriate responses e.g. teaching a child how to stroke a cat by holding their hand to regulate the movement.
- **Environmental management**: We should be constantly looking for ways to improve the environment in which we work and the service user lives. Environments should be adapted and modified to meet the individual needs of people e.g. lighting/decor/furnishings.
- **Skill Teaching**: Support service users with skill building e.g. helping service users to function independently, enabling them to cope with their emotions and to communicate effectively.

Positive behaviour should be reinforced so that the individual feels that when they are managing well, this is noticed and recognised. We respond well to positive reinforcement and will seek those good feelings again, and this may also allow us to aim further to achieve our goals.

All the strategies and techniques utilised need to have a service wide and consistent approach. This is important as not only does it set a standard for how support staff will work with an individual, it also offers reassurance to the individual that staff understand the needs of those they are supporting and how best to achieve this. It allows for the safety and security of everyone involved.

It is vital to evaluate how effective plans are and be open to adjustment to ensure that each plan is as effective as possible. Any strategy needs to be regularly reviewed and updated where necessary to ensure that it is still able to meet the requirements and that it is fit for purpose.

Aversive/Non-aversive Approaches

PBS is focussed on utilising non-aversive strategies to support behavioural changes instead of aversive approaches.
- Non-aversive behaviour management promotes techniques that avoid consequences that punish a behaviour
- Aversive behaviour management techniques may cause the person discomfort, or they may find the consequences unpleasant, causing them to try to escape or avoid the outcome

When developing management plans we should always look at non-aversive strategies first, examples of non-aversive strategies include:
- Positive reinforcement
- Praise
- Distraction
- Engagement
- Modelling and shaping
- Prompts, hints and cueing
- Exercise
- Intensive interaction
- Environmental change

Aversive behaviour management includes, but is not limited to:
- Manual restraint
- Mechanical restraint
- Time out/sending to isolate
- Medical restraint such as PRN
- Removal or restriction of favoured items/activities

Looking again at how we might react to the aversive strategies we can understand the negative impact they would have on a positive working relationship. When used as primary methods of behaviour management they do not enhance the quality of life and will often lead to further and maybe more intense behaviours as a response.

We all respond better to positives so it is easy to understand why these strategies will benefit not only the individual but also those that are supporting them. By continuing to utilise non-aversive techniques we can continue to build positive working relationships with the individual to help reduce the effect and occurrence of challenging or disruptive behaviours.

Secondary Strategies Including De-escalation

Secondary Strategies focus on the individual's early behavioural signs (physical, emotional, communicative, etc.), which can indicate an increase in behavioural disturbance.

These strategies are designed to aid early intervention and help prevent further escalation.

Recognising Changes in Behaviour

When we notice a change in a person's mood or behaviour, our response is key to the management of that situation. Within a behaviour management plan will be listed ways in which to engage and de-escalate the individual. Getting this stage right is paramount to preventing further escalation.

You should acknowledge any change in mood and take positive action as soon as you are aware there is a potential problem or distress. This may simply mean distracting him/her or changing the tone of the discussion. Sometimes all you have to do is listen and acknowledge his/her feelings.

Signs you may notice when an individual's behaviour changes include:
- Changes in their body language
- Agitation
- Red, flushed faced
- Sweaty
- Fixed eye contact
- Making strange/loud/repetitive noises
- Head banging
- Refusal to co-operate or communicate

Challenging behaviour generally follows a pattern that increases in scale from the baseline behaviour of an individual, where a person is displaying what would be established as "normal" for them, through various stages which may include frustrated, distressed, angry or aggressive, to violent or crisis point.

Any sign that a person's base-line behaviour is changing and escalating towards challenging behaviour should prompt us to implement the prescribed intervention as described in their person centred plan.

Any interactive intervention will need good communication at its core.

How We Communicate

General communication follows a process called Transactional Analysis.
- A message is formed by the sender
- The message is sent to the recipient using verbal and non-verbal communication
- The message is received and de-coded by the recipient
- The recipient chooses a response

Problems can arise if the communication at either end is not effective, for example, if the sender speaks one language and the recipient another, the message can be lost in translation and the response may not be appropriate. This helps us understand the need for effective communication when supporting a person, particularly a person with a learning disability or physical impairment such as hearing loss.

This is highlighted even more when we understand that a person's behaviour can change their perception of a situation, leading to further misunderstanding.

It is important that you give out the right messages. People generally read your true feelings by observing how you appear and act, by listening to what you say and how you say it in the following proportions:
- The words used 7%
- Tone of voice 38%
- Body language 55%

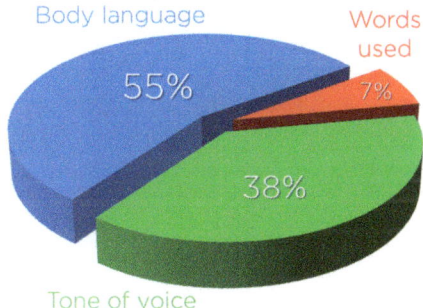

Source: British Journal of Clinical and Social Psychology

You can see from these percentages that 93% of how a person judges your mood and attitude is through your body language and tone of voice.

By monitoring your own responses and non-verbal communication you will help avoid causing any further distress.

Barriers to Communication

To successfully de-escalate a situation, we need to be aware of any barriers to communication and how we can overcome them. These will be specific to the person and be included as part of their person centred management plan.

Barriers to communication include, but are not limited to:
- Pain/discomfort
- Stress
- Alcohol/drugs
- Fatigue
- Language/jargon
- Cultural differences
- Educational background
- Light levels/background noise/activity
- Physical or mental health
- Self-perception/status of others
- Current message conflicts with previous message

Overcoming Barriers to Communication

Some individuals with severe speech disorders cannot effectively communicate verbally and rely on other methods of communication instead. Methods such as: gestures, body language, formal sign language, writing, electronic or visual aids. These methods are used to enhance or provide an alternative means of communication.

Gestures and Body Language

Gestures and body language can be used in tandem with speech to get a message across. Examples of this are: pointing to objects, giving the "thumbs up", winking, crossing the arms, shaking or nodding the head. These are all means of conveying a message, other than or in addition to speaking.

Unfortunately, gestures and body language are not universal, nor are they standardised. What might be a gesture with a specific reason or message to one person may have a totally different meaning to another.

The same could also be applied across cultural divides. When communicating with someone who relies on gestures or body language to augment their verbal speech, we should take care to learn what each gesture or action means. Gestures may also be difficult for individuals on the Autistic Spectrum to understand as they may find these distracting from the words when used in combination.

Sign Language

This method of communication uses hand signs to convey meanings. Sign language may be used to augment verbal communication, but is often an alternative means of communication. Sometimes described as "talking with the hands", many people are referred to as being able to speak through sign language. Facial expressions, finger spellings and shoulder movements also comprise methods of communicating via sign language.

Communication Aids

A variety of communication aids exist to either augment or replace verbal speech where necessary e.g. electronic, computer software, text to speech, voice amplifiers, word/symbol boards or cards (the boards or cards allow individuals to point to words or symbols that they wish to communicate).

Ensuring Effective Communication

The following are ways of ensuring more effective communication:
- Keep an open mind. Question WHY there is misunderstanding or frustration
- Communicate at an appropriate eye level
- Ensure a "low arousal" approach, moderate eye contact, volume, touch, proximity
- Remember service users may have difficulty understanding abstract concepts, time and negatives
- Speak slowly, clearly and calmly using simple direct words and phrases. Give service users time to process the message
- Clarify any points and CHECK understanding. Repeat or re-phrase if necessary
- Use key words, objects, Makaton, pictures, tapes, videos or any other aids that may help

- Service users may agree with you because it is easier. Ensure they are given opportunity to express their real needs
- Maintain a non-judgemental approach and don't make assumptions; remember challenging behaviour always happens for a reason; believe a positive outcome is possible; and accept that sometimes our best efforts may fail through no fault of our own.

De-escalation

Whilst there is no script on how to de-escalate a situation there are key skills that can be utilised to support effective de-escalation. Here are a few examples using the acronym DE-ESCALATION:

D = **Distraction:** can the individuals' attention be focussed on something else?
E = **Encourage:** positive behaviour/responses
E = **Empathise:** try and see the situation from the other person's perspective
S = **Space:** think about how the other person might be affected by your presence or proximity
C = **Calm:** you must try to remain calm if only in appearance
A = **Attitude:** maintain a positive attitude
L = **Listen:** actively and allow them time to process and answer
A = **Assertiveness:** take control but do not become aggressive
T = **Team work:** use the skills of your team effectively
I = **Intuition:** use your intuition and be prepared to act if you feel unsafe
O = **Openness:** be open and honest and admit it if something has gone wrong
N = **Negotiation:** be prepared to keep negotiating if this helps prevent the use of restrictive alternatives

De-escalation can be looked at in three phases, the Calming Phase, Building Rapport and Reaching a Positive Conclusion.

Calming Phase

To begin to de-escalate a difficult situation you must first instil an element of calm. Acknowledge the service user's feelings and mood. Respect their personal space and take a step-back if necessary.

Adopt a relaxed posture and engage with them using a calm, neutral tone of voice. It may help to remove any audience or move away from other people (where possible and if safe to do so), avoid environments that may trigger further behavioural escalation e.g. noisy or over active areas.

Building Rapport

Try to empathise with them. Be sure to use an appropriate level of communication, explain things clearly and then carefully observe visual cues and use those cues to respond as appropriate. Listen actively to the service user and think about the questions you need to ask them; allow them time to understand your questions and form a response. Continue to use a calm, neutral voice throughout the process and be prepared to offer alternative choices to help resolve the issue.

Reaching a Positive Conclusion

Where possible follow the Positive Behaviour Management Plan. If this is not working, consider liaising with a colleague and allow them to take over. Consider caring interventions aimed at calming or reducing arousal levels; these may include diversion and distraction techniques. You may need to outline the boundaries for acceptable behaviour. In some situations, it can be effective to use strategic capitulation, give the person what they want at that time to prevent having to take actions that carry a greater risk.

Reactions to Challenging Behaviour

When faced with challenging behaviour it is natural for our body to experience increased levels of stress. Being involved in a confrontation is never easy but the way we respond will depend on our past experiences and the severity of the incident. Understanding how our body can react can help us to prepare for the impact an incident might have on us both physically and emotionally.

The human body responds to the increase in stress by releasing adrenaline into the blood stream. The following is a list of possible reactions that can result from this increase of adrenaline:
- Pounding heart
- Dry mouth
- Shaking/Jelly legs
- Muscular tension
- Breathing faster
- Feeling nausea or sick
- Churning stomach
- Sense of panic
- Indecisiveness
- Freezing
- Feeling not in control
- Feeling weak
- Lost for words
- Raised temperature
- A feeling of anger or indignation

It is reassuring to know that everyone suffers from some or all of these symptoms to some degree, including the person who is being angry or aggressive.

This rush of adrenaline will also affect your ability to reason with common sense. The brain is less able to control rational thought and is more prone to instinctive responses during the adrenaline rush. It is crucial that you try to appear calm when under pressure and remain in control of your own responses:
- Control your breathing: slow it down by breathing out slowly
- Try to relax your muscles and think positive thoughts
- Step back if necessary and think about your position and stance
- Try to focus on the problem and not on how you feel

Once the perceived danger is no longer present, the brain signals the release of noradrenaline to help the body return to normal. Breathing slows and becomes deeper, the heart rate slows down, muscles relax, vision returns to normal to include peripheral vision, and the blood is diverted back to all normal bodily requirements including to the more rational and conscious parts of the brain.

How Attitude Affects Behaviour

Despite how you might be feeling you should try to appear composed and assertive. You should try to look confident, as if you are capable of dealing with the situation. You should control your voice and use measured tones; this should help bring the situation to a satisfactory conclusion.

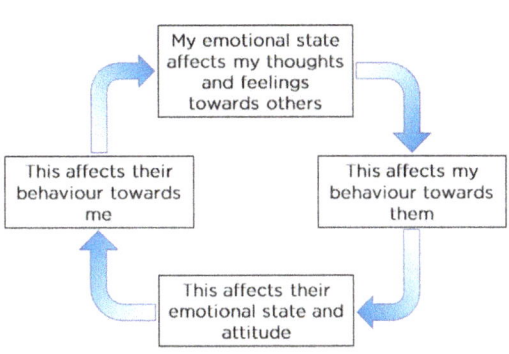

At the very least it should prevent escalation.

If you fail to control your response you could end up becoming part of the problem. You may say or do something which inflames the situation and that you later regret.

The person being aggressive may attempt to justify an escalation of their behaviour if they can provoke a negative or angry response from you. It is essential that you maintain a positive approach and attitude, as this will influence your thoughts and behaviour, which in turn will influence the attitude and behaviour of the service user.

Tertiary Strategies Including Physical Intervention

Tertiary strategies are used when an actual behaviour of concern is presenting, with the primary aim to bring the incident to an end in a timely and safe manner, with due regard to the individual's rights and dignity.

These strategies can be separated into two categories:
1. **Non-restrictive Intervention**: including de-escalation, diversion, distraction or strategic capitulation (covered in the last section)

2. **Restrictive Intervention:** verbal e.g. "you can't have it"; physical e.g. holding someone preventing free movement; chemical e.g. sedation; mechanical e.g. harnesses or splints; environmental e.g. seclusion, baffle door handles, blocking a doorway
"Any intervention used to limit a person's liberty" (RCN; 2006)

Restrictive Physical Intervention and the Law

The subject and issue of Restraint and Restrictive Physical Intervention is one that is widely debated across the UK (and elsewhere). The use of physical interventions in response to the challenging behaviour of people with Autism and other associated complex needs is not an approach which gains much support, except as part of an overall strategy and as a last resort and only when all other non-aversive approaches have been tried and failed, and when there really is no other alternative.

People with Autistic Spectrum Disorder (ASD) and associated complex needs have a right to be treated with respect, care and dignity, including times when they behave in ways that may be harmful to themselves or others, and where physical intervention from staff is required. It is imperative staff working with people with learning disabilities and ASD (which present challenging behaviour) are equipped with the right skills. Employers have a duty to provide appropriate training to those individuals who work in these environments.

Staff need to have a knowledge and understanding of the relevant legislation and guidance enabling them to act appropriately, effectively and in a safe manner when dealing with difficult situations.

Defining Restrictive Physical Intervention

There is no single definition for restraint or physical intervention that is universally accepted within or across the different professions. This can leave staff unsure as to what constitutes restraint or physical intervention and/or how to define their practice(s) in some situations. Available definitions include:

> *"A degree of direct physical force to limit or restrict movement or mobility"*
> (bild (1996), Physical Interventions: A policy framework)

> "A set of physical interventions which may be used to control an individual whose behaviour may be injurious to himself or others and with whom non-physical intervention, for example, communication, de-escalation and problem solving skills have been unsuccessful."
> (East London and The City Mental Health Trust, policy on Physical Restraint)
>
> "A skilled hands-on method of physical restraint involving trained designated healthcare professionals to prevent individuals from harming themselves, endangering others or seriously compromising the therapeutic environment. Its purpose is to safely immobilise the individual concerned."
> (National Institute for Clinical Excellence (NICE), Definition of Physical Interventions)

Care Quality Commission Essential Standards of Quality and Safety 2010 (Part 2: Guidance 7F) states:
"People who use services or receive care, treatment and support from staff who, in relation to restraint:
- Know and understand the different forms that restraint can take.
- Understand when different types of restraint are or are not appropriate, prioritising de-escalation or positive behaviour support over restraint whenever possible.
- Understand that restraint should be used in a way that respects dignity and protects human rights wherever possible.
- Know whether and what type of restraint is permitted in the service in which they work.
- Understanding that restraint should only be used as a last resort, and that the type of restraint should be the least restrictive and for the minimum amount of time to ensure harm is prevented and that the person, and others around them, are safe."

Where Physical Force is Used to Prevent Injury

Ultimately, in a Court of Law, it is the Criminal Law Act (1967) that will be used to determine if the force used was reasonable.

Section 3 of the Criminal Law Act (1967) provides:
"A person may use such force as is reasonable in the circumstances..."

This applies to those events that are in progress and to those that "reasonably appear to be about to be committed".

What is Reasonable Force?

The term reasonable force is seen as vague; there are criteria which must be met to establish that where force has been used, it was done so to stop a perceived threat in the least restrictive and safest way.

When establishing whether the actions were reasonable, certain questions must be answered in terms of the use of force, were your actions:
- **Necessary**: Were all other options exhausted, or proven to be impractical or ineffective? Would taking no action result in significant harm? Did you follow the guidelines, policies and behaviour management plans?
- **Proportionate**: Was the force used proportionate to the risk presented? Was size, numbers, age, weapons, prior history of violence considered in your response? Did you use the least restrictive approach?
- **Time Limited**: Was the force used for the minimum amount of time to ensure the threat was no longer present?

Least Restrictive Approach

A "least restrictive approach" might help staff to justify and defend their actions by demonstrating that:
- All other options were explored and failed, or that the alternatives were deemed to be unsuitable for the level of risk presented
- The minimum amount of force was used for the minimum amount of time
- The staff response was professionally and legally defensible

Any plan that involves physical intervention and restrictions should be risk assessed for the individual and only include the techniques that are approved for use. When determining risk, we need to factor in all of the information we have based on the person, including any physical limitations they may have and medical diagnosis. We also need to consider professional opinion and lived experience to highlight risks that may be presented during their use.

Risk assessments must identify:
- The nature of the hazard and the potential for harm
- The factors that increase the likelihood of staff exposure to the hazard
- The measures necessary to eliminate, reduce or manage the hazard

The appropriate qualified person(s) should carry out a systematic analysis of actual and potential risks. This can be used to develop care plans that ensure working practices, operating systems and safety checks are adequate, correct and meet the service user's needs. Staff should not consider using restraint unless the appropriate risk assessment has been completed and documented within the individual care plan.

Risks of Physical Intervention

Along with the fact that restricting another person's freedom has an impact on their human rights, dignity and feelings of respect, there are other risks to consider when including any physical intervention as part of a management strategy.
- Could the intervention cause discomfort and distress to the individual?
- Does the restriction make the individual relive past experiences?
- What psychological affect does the physical intervention have on the individual?
- Could the Physical Intervention result in pain or injury?
- Will the use of Physical Intervention have an impact on the relationship between them and those there to support them?
- Is the use of Physical Intervention becoming routine instead of as a last resort?
- Is there a risk of abuse of power by staff?

Asphyxia

When considering the use of physical intervention, we need to understand the risks associated with breathing. In terms of our context we can look at the following:
- Positional Asphyxia occurs when the position of the individual prevents them from breathing adequately
- Restraint Asphyxia occurs when the position of the individual prevents them from breathing adequately and as a result of physical restraint the person cannot get out of that position

For a person's respiratory system to function they need the following 3 elements of anatomy to be free to work properly:

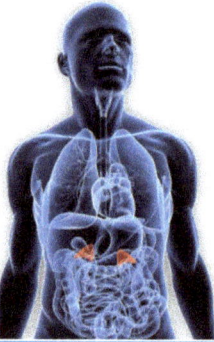

1. The Airway must be clear to allow oxygen in and out of the lungs.

2. The Chest must be able to expand to allow the lungs to inflate.

3. The Diaphragm has to be able to contract to increase lung capacity.

If one or more of these elements is compromised, we will either have difficulty taking in oxygen or difficulty expelling carbon dioxide and other gases causing breathing difficulties.

Circumstances when asphyxia may occur are, when a person is:
- Laid in a prone position (face down) on their stomach and pressure is applied to their back
- "Doubled" forward in the seated position restricting movement of the diaphragm
- Has pressure applied to the neck, head or torso during restraint
- Mechanically restrained (belts, straps, handcuffs) and is left unattended
- Confined in a position that restricts breathing and that they cannot escape from

The risk of asphyxia occurring is heightened if:
- The person is intoxicated with alcohol, medication or drugs
- The person is suffering from respiratory problems or fatigue
- The person is overweight or overheated
- The person has previously exerted/exhausted themselves through violent activity such as struggling or fighting

What to look out for:
- Gurgling or gasping sounds
- Breathing that is laboured or distressed
- Verbal complaints or difficulty speaking
- An increased effort to struggle or distress/anxiety
- A violent or loud person suddenly changes to a passive, quiet and tranquil one
- Pale/grey/blue skin colouring to the lips, nail beds or earlobes, then to the face and other parts of the body

Do not assume that because a person is snoring that they are asleep
You can reduce the risk of asphyxia by:
- Avoid putting direct pressure on the back, chest or stomach area of a person during restraint
- When a person has been restrained, get them to a seated, kneeling or standing position as soon as possible
- Reduce the level of intervention as soon as possible
- Consider alternative strategies to prolonged or regular physical intervention, e.g. environmental or medical interventions
- Where possible avoid floor restraint. Releasing the person and re-engaging with them in the kneeling or standing positions are less hazardous
- Transport people in a seated position; never face down on their stomach
- Monitor the condition/life signs of the person continually
- Get medical assistance immediately if you have any concerns about the condition of the person

Recording Physical Interventions

When recording the use of any physical intervention there is an increased need for specifics. The information in these reports needs to include:

- What was each staff member doing? E.g. managing the left arm with support hold whilst talking to the person in an attempt to de-escalate
- What techniques were being used?
- How did the individual respond to the engagement of staff in physical intervention? E.g. did they struggle, relax, become verbally aggressive?
- How long did the intervention last? Was each stage/level used for the minimum length of time and reduced as soon as possible?
- What was said during the restriction? Exact wording should be used, as with any record keeping, as this increases the understanding of the individual's behaviour
- Any recordable injuries?

Following an incident staff need to record the facts, clearly and concisely so that any occurrences of challenging behaviour can be looked at with a view to utilising other strategies that are non-restrictive. It also allows the review of current practices and will highlight any areas that need improvement. We also need to be sure that if the use of physical intervention is increasing then there may be a cultural issue within the setting that needs to be addressed.

Post Incident Procedures

Support for all those involved should be a priority, not just for the medical aspect, in terms of any injuries, but also the psychological impact. Recording and reporting the incident using current guidelines and legislation should be carried out post incident. Recording what has happened allows us to carry out a review and to apply what we have learnt to better support individuals in times of distress.

There are numerous reasons why it is important to document incidents including:
- Legal obligation: including the Care Act, Health and Safety legislation, Mental Capacity Act, Mental Health Act
- To highlight patterns of behaviour, frequency of behaviour, potential causes of behaviour
- Develop management strategies
- Monitor current policies and procedures
- Provide protection for service users and staff
- To highlight any training and development needs for staff

Incident reviews should be carried out by a multi-disciplinary team to ensure the management of the incident was appropriate and where it is found not to have been, investigations should be carried out following local and national guidelines.

Post Incident Support

Everyone involved in an incident will feel some impact as a result. They may have feelings of negative emotions or crying, low mood or depression, elation and excitement. Physical effects may include: shock, headaches, nausea or being sick. These feelings are not limited to staff involved; it also includes the service user and witnesses. It is important that everyone involved, including the service users, are given the appropriate support after the event.

Following an incident, we need to conduct a de-brief which includes the individual when they have returned to their baseline behaviour and are receptive. If we attempt this too soon, we can often trigger a further escalation in behaviour.

Other types of support available could include:
- **Counselling:** Informal or formal counselling, speaking one-to-one with staff or colleagues or in groups (such as staff meetings etc). Formal counselling could take place in the form of supervised sessions with occupational services or other outside agencies
- **Time-out:** People may simply need to take a break or change their surroundings by taking time out, or in certain cases staff may need to go home
- **Change of Duties:** Staff may feel that they need to change their role, temporarily or permanently. Where this is practical, employer support should be given
- **Restorative Practice:** Where there is a need to build/rebuild relationships, restorative practice should be considered. Generally, this may involve professionals including but not limited to Psychologists, Speech and Language Therapists and Advocates, as well as those involved directly with the situation

The Service User Perspective

The service user has the right to have their views and opinions heard and responded to. We should listen to what they say (or communicate) and take their views seriously. We should provide information in such a way that they feel safe and understand what may happen to them if they become challenging or violent.

Make them aware of their rights and what they can do if they feel the need to complain. Where it is possible negotiate the intervention strategy with the service user. Where necessary, provide access to independent or external advocacy.

Conclusion

You cannot always prevent incidents occurring; in some environments they are part of the routine. When faced with challenging behaviour many outcomes are possible. You will have achieved a positive outcome if no one can accuse you of contributing to the problem, or of "making things worse".

Reflection and Reflective Practice

One of the most effective ways of continually developing person centred care plans in a way that prevents challenging behaviour reoccurring, or better prepares us to deal with it next time, is by reflecting on past experiences. It is important to review events and ask questions about the situation, the way it was managed and what the outcomes were. It is also important that we do not use this review as a tool to focus on the negative aspects of the situation or to point out negative performance.

Some questions we might want to ask:
- How did the situation start?
- What was I doing at the time?
- What were my colleagues doing at the time?
- What exactly happened?
- How did I feel at the time?
- Think about what was done well and what did not go well.
- How did the situation come to an end?
- What could I do differently next time?

Below are 2 common examples of reflective practice.

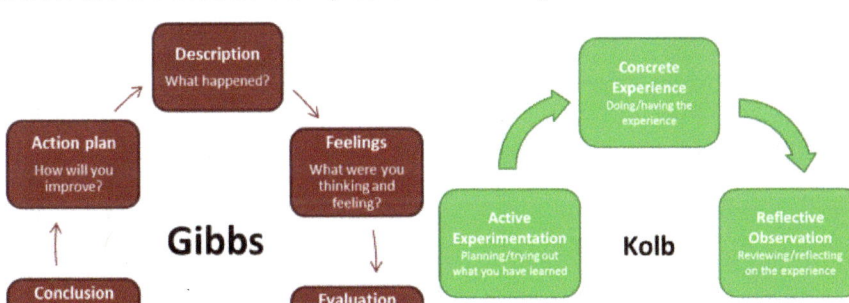

Both of these models help us to analyse an event in a way that enables us to learn from our experiences and will help us plan for future events and be better prepared to manage them the next time we are faced with the same dilemma.

Summary

All services that provide care and support to adults with ASD and associated complex needs should be sensitive to each individual's needs and respect their cultural, ethnic and sexual background.

When considering the need to use any form of restrictive intervention, a detailed assessment must be carried out in such a way that it is completely "person centred".

It must take into account all aspects of the individual and must indicate necessity as well as advocating "best interest criteria".

Restrictive physical interventions will only ever be considered when all other options have been exhausted. They need to have been fully risk assessed and deemed as being in the person's best interests following a multi-disciplinary process.

Individualised procedures should be established for responding to service users who are likely to present challenging or hazardous behaviour. This may be in the delivery of day to day care procedures or due to behavioural problems that may compromise the safety and wellbeing of others.

Services follow a graded approach to any intervention procedure. They will always follow the option of last resort when considering the need to use any restrictive physical intervention.

References

Adults with Incapacity Act (Scotland) 2000
Autism Act 2009
Care Act 2014
Care Standards Act (National Minimum Standards for Children's Homes) 2000
Children Act (Scotland) 1995
Children and Families Act 2014
Children and Social Work Act 2017
Children's Act 1989
Children's Act 2004
Criminal Justice Act 2003
Criminal Law Act (Northern Ireland) 1967
Deprivation of Liberty Act 2010
Education Act 1996
Education and Inspections Act 2006
Education (Scotland) Act 1980 ch47
Equality Act 2010
Health and Safety at Work Act 1974
Human Rights Act 1998
Mental Capacity Act 2005
Mental Capacity Act (Northern Ireland) 2016
Mental Health Act 2003
Mental Health Act 2007
Mental Health (Care and Treatment) (Scotland) Act 2003
Mental Health Units (Use of Force) Act 2018
National Health Service Act 2006 sch 4
Protection of Children Act 1999
Regulation of Care (Scotland) Act 2001

Notes

Notes

www.ingramcontent.com/pod-product-compliance
Lightning Source LLC
Chambersburg PA
CBHW062114290426
44110CB00023B/2810